Ministering to Addicts

Trudy Makepeace

malcolm down

PUBLISHING

First published 2022 by Malcolm Down Publishing Ltd
www.malcolmdown.co.uk

24 23 22 22   7 6 5 4 3 2 1

British Library Cataloguing in Publication Data
A catalogue record for this book is available from the British Library.

ISBN 978-1-915046-23-9

Cover design by <???>
Art direction by Sarah Grace

Printed in the UK

Contents

Introduction

This booklet has been written to help inform ministers, churches and other Christian organisations that seek to open their doors and hearts to those who find themselves struggling with or recovering from addiction.

This booklet is by no means exhaustive but as a former addict of 18 years I share personal insights from my own journey, as one who has experienced healing and freedom. I bring this together with what I learned and encountered as a support worker and then manager of a Christian rehabilitation centre in South Wales, and recently as an outreach worker and evangelist.

Whilst there is not one prescriptive pathway to see people step into and maintain freedom, I believe the things I cover here are all vital to the individual's ongoing freedom and recovery. My hope is to bring insight and confidence as you support others on this journey.

The power of the Gospel

The gospel . . . is the power of God that brings salvation to everyone who believes. (Romans 1:16)

The gospel message has not changed and it continues to transform the human heart, bringing hope, healing, and purpose to all who receive salvation in Jesus' name.

This includes the sick, the broken in spirit and in heart, those troubled and tormented, the oppressed, the demonised, and all those who are without Christ.

Jesus heals and sets captives free

The Spirit of the Lord is on me, because he has anointed me to proclaim good news to the poor. He has sent me to proclaim freedom for the prisoners and recovery of sight for the blind, to set the oppressed free, to proclaim the year of the Lord's favour. (Luke 4:18-19)

Jesus had compassion on the sick and all those who were oppressed. He went around healing and delivering those afflicted and held captive by all kinds of strongholds, for God was with Him (Acts 10:38).

Addiction

Addiction is a stronghold. Addiction is the fact or condition of being addicted to a particular substance or activity.

Drug and alcohol addiction is an epidemic not only here in the West but all over the world; it has become part of our cultural landscape. It is important to recognise that addiction is not just about substance and alcohol abuse, but can also include lust, pornography, sex, adultery, gambling, stealing, shopping, materialism, medication, money, social status, work, sugar, food, self-harm, computer games, social media and much more.

However, drugs and alcohol tend to be more outwardly noticeable because there is often a more dramatic change in physical appearance, behaviour, and emotional well-being.

Drug and alcohol addiction

Drug abuse and alcohol addiction is now known and understood to be a brain disease as it alters the mind. It affects the structure of the brain and how it works. This can be seen in harmful behaviours that addicts display.[1]

Addiction is born out of choices, not that one chooses to become an addict, but these choices are often influenced by and associated with trauma and/or unhealthy childhood experiences which were not within the child's control. An ongoing repetition of a poor choice, in this example of using alcohol and drugs, leads into dependency. Consequently,

---

1. https://www.drugabuse.gov/publications/drugs-brains-behavior-science-addiction/drugs-brain provides helpful insight as to how drugs can alter and affect an individual's brain.

the chosen substance often gets its hook into people before they are aware of it.

Addiction blocks and inhibits new learning and affects the brain's ability to make good, healthy, and responsible choices. It alters the way the brain thinks. It also stunts emotional growth and maturity. For the addict their substance of choice increasingly becomes the focus and driving force in their life. As their addiction increases their obsession increases. This means their cognitive skills are increasingly impaired and, therefore, the ability to take control and make good choices. Gradually they become enslaved. At that point addiction becomes a life-threatening issue as subsequent behaviours become more erratic and irrational, leading to harmful and dangerous consequences which affect them physically, mentally, and emotionally.

Common behaviour and traits of addicts

Being aware of some of these behavioural characteristics can help all parties. For the person ministering it can help them to be more assertive, which will also aid the person being ministered to as opposed to allowing the behaviours to continue.

- Self-loathing often connected to guilt and shame

- Victim mentality

- Deceit/denial

- Manipulation

- Selfishness

- Violence and aggression

- Criminal activity

Factors which commonly contribute to struggles with addiction

It can be easy to fall into judging those with addictions, but often those addictions have been born out of difficult and complex challenges such as:

- Abuse

- Childhood neglect

- Trauma

- Loss and bereavement

- Poverty

- Peer pressure

- Influence of others and environment (lack of ability to make good choices and boundaries)

- Seeking fulfilment and pleasure to fill a void in their hearts and lives

- Trying to sustain a level of 'normality'; as the addiction progresses it becomes about being able to function

Common psychological and emotional effects of addiction

The list below shows how powerful and extreme the effects of addiction can be on a person's mental and emotional well-being.

- Mood swings and paranoia

- Violence

- Cravings

- Extreme pleasure

- Mental health deteriorates

- Depression

- Hallucinations

- Confusion

- Engaging with increasingly risky behaviour

- Self-sabotage

- Physiological tolerance to a substance grows creating a desire for ever-increasing amounts

- Withdrawals

- Stunts growth, emotional maturity, and the ability to cope with responsibility

- Strengthens ungodly beliefs and strongholds

- Attitudes of entitlement and rebellion

- The transfer of one addiction for another

Some physical effects of addiction

These will often be more evident in prolonged addiction:

- Malnutrition

- Sickness and poor immune system

- Cravings

- Physical dependency leading to withdrawals when deprived of substance (commonly identified as 'going cold turkey'): abdominal pain, vomiting, shakes, fever, diarrhoea

- Psychological dependency

- Risk of contracting hepatitis, HIV, and other illnesses due to injecting, sharing paraphernalia, or having unprotected sex

- Heart rate irregularities, heart attacks

- Kidney and liver damage resulting from alcohol abuse

- Seizures, stroke, brain damage

- Changes in appetite, body temperature, and sleep patterns

Some social effects of addiction for the addict

Whilst there are many challenges for society dealing with addiction and its repercussions, the addict is often oblivious to them or becomes desensitised and accepts these effects as their 'normal'. This can be a major challenge to their mindset and ability to change.

- Poverty

- Breakdown and loss of relationships and families

- Isolation

- Unable to maintain work or function normally in society

- Loss of accommodation

- Disconnected from communities

- Drug-related crime

- Domestic violence

The call to reach addicts with the gospel

Addiction is now so widespread that most families will be affected in some way through some form of addiction. No one wakes up one day thinking, 'I will become an addict.' Everyone is someone's son or daughter. Every addict is a human being loved by God.

Jesus is our ultimate example. Jesus calls us to go just as He did, into the highways and the byways, to those who are on the margins of society, to bring them the good news of the Kingdom (Luke 14:23).

It is important that we understand and recognise, just as Jesus did, that people are individuals, from varied backgrounds, each with their own unique journey and story, no two people are the same. To be able to connect and truly have any significant impact and influence upon people's lives for Christ, we must also grow in our awareness and understanding of the times, culture, and issues that those in our communities and nations face. This will enable us to be more effective in partnering with God and His purposes as we seek to serve, minister, and come alongside people in an authentic way.

The apostle Paul said he became all things to all people so that some may be saved (1 Corinthians 9:22). Let love lead you, meet the individual where they are, journey with them. Walk alongside them, build them up, encourage them in their hopes and goals.

Three keys to unlocking opportunities to connect with addicts

1. Love – Love overcomes. Love believes all things and hopes all things; love perseveres, and love breaks down barriers. It's the love of God in us that compels us and helps us to go on loving a person despite their struggle. The act of love and the language of love sees and values the person despite any negative or challenging behaviour and difficulties.

2. Authenticity – Keeping it real in your own life and in your interactions with others. None of us are without

fault. Remaining humble and truthful and being straightforward will be a powerful witness that may lead to those in addiction encountering Jesus.

3. Non-judgemental – Fear of judgement may be one of the biggest barriers to an addict coming to God, walking into a church, or continuing with God if they are struggling. They will already have judged themselves unworthy. Discovering their value may be the very thing to release them from their own judgement and enable them to discover God's love and forgiveness.

It is these essentials that will enable you to connect with addicts, bringing a demonstration of the person, presence, and power of Christ to all that you minister to.

Why people may fear reaching out to those in addiction

You or others you know may feel some nervousness when thinking about working with addicts. This is completely normal, and if you can recognise the root of these fears, they are easier to overcome.

- A lack of understanding or experience

- Lack of physical and emotional safety

- Blaming the addict

- Prejudice and anger towards the addict

- Unsure how to communicate with those affected

- Unable to control the situation or fix it

- Intimidated by erratic behaviours or their appearance

- Destructive behaviour

- Unsure how to minister appropriately

- Erratic behaviours damage relationships and can wreak havoc for all involved

Anointed ones

As God's children we are called and chosen as God's anointed ones: those who carry Jesus' presence, power, and authority over the works of darkness. This enables the children of God to minister to people to see them saved, healed, and delivered.

Behold, I give you the authority to trample on serpents and scorpions, and over all the power of the enemy, and nothing shall by any means hurt you. (Luke 10:19 NKJV)

Testimonies of exercising authority

One woman called Jo came into Street Church, a ministry I run. She was a self-harmer, suicidal, and despairing. After coming for a while, getting to know us and listening to the messages week by week, one day she responded to receive Jesus. Afterwards she shared how she immediately stopped self-harming and no longer felt suicidal. Her journey of healing has been messy and she has had some setbacks but she has not self-harmed or been plagued with thoughts of suicide since; the power of the enemy to harm her was broken.

I encountered Sharon during an outreach. She was talking to herself and to others that we could not see. She was aggressive in her manner, angrily shouting and swearing uncontrollably. This was evident as her behaviour switched: one minute she was calm as we spoke to her and then she would switch to extreme, vulgar, non-stop outbursts. Her eyes were also an indicator of something much darker at work. I discerned through our conversation and observing her behaviour that as well as some obvious mental health issues and alcoholism issues, there were also demonic influences at work in her life. As she continued with her aggressive, vile language and accusations, I quietly took authority over the spirit at work and prayed. I commanded the spirit to stop, by taking authority in Jesus' name.

Prayer example: *I take authority over every filthy and tormenting spirit in the name of Jesus Christ and command you to stop. In Jesus' name I forbid you to operate. I speak peace over her now in Jesus' name.*

Several times I quietly commanded the 'unclean spirit' to shut up until she calmed down, at which point I was then able to talk to Sharon herself without the added distraction of the demonic interference. She then stopped cursing and being vile and came close, enabling me to talk to her for a short while before the interference returned. In her case she needed deliverance. What's more, she had complex mental health needs and it was inappropriate in that instance to attempt any deliverance without her first receiving Christ as her Lord and Saviour, or knowing more about her situation.

Whether you are experienced with working in the field of addiction and mental health or not, we can all learn, and we can all listen. As followers of Jesus we can seek discernment and His wisdom in all situations.

Understanding the power of addiction

When someone becomes addicted the object of their addiction becomes an idol in their life. It becomes their god and obtains the worship of their mind, body, and soul. The nature of addiction is self-gratifying and obsessive, which leads to a place where the addict becomes in danger of being possessed by their addiction. This was my experience: I was under the complete control and influence of drugs. The more I gave in to the compelling urges to use, the more enslaved I became, and the more destructive behaviour and heartache followed.

The Bible warns that the sorrow of those that run after false gods will multiply (Psalm 16:4) and that we will become enslaved by the things that we worship.

The good news is that the power of Jesus' blood shed on the cross breaks the curse of sin and its work in our lives.

As a former addict I know the reality of that power because Jesus broke the control and curse of sin in my life. He broke the chains of my addiction that had me bound for 18 years. Jesus rescued me and lifted me up out of a horrible pit, and His resurrection power raised me from spiritual death to a new life in Christ. From the moment I was saved, I discovered a life of victory over sin and addiction.

Understanding the battle

It is important to understand that whilst it is true that there are many former addicts with stories of radical transformation, it is the journey of walking in their new-found freedom that is essential to break the habits and strongholds that influence their mind and emotions. Often these will underline in some way the choice to use. Those patterns of wrong thinking that have been influenced negatively by culture, by the personal influence of others, and one's own experiences growing up that go on to lead people into places of limitation, captivity, and hopelessness.

The principle of renewing is found in Romans 12:2, and it is vital for an individual to enter the fullness of the freedom that Christ died to give them.

And do not be conformed to this world, but be transformed by the renewing of your mind, that you may prove what is that good and acceptable and perfect will of God. (Romans 12:2 NKJV)

Even in secular society, part of the cure to addiction is believed to be 'cognitive change' i.e. changing the way that you think.

Whilst drug treatments may work for some people, ultimately the transformation of the inner person and healing of the mind and heart comes from a living relationship with God. After 33 attempts to get and remain clean, my experience of freedom from addiction has been born out of His transformation of my heart and mind, that has come from making Jesus Christ the Lord of my life. Turning from my old ways to follow Him and His ways.

Freedom comes and is maintained though relationship with Jesus and the renewal of the mind through the word of God. This process of renewing the mind brings about a greater revelation of truth. It tears down lies and strongholds that have set themselves up in the mind of the believer. Discovering and receiving those truths mean that individuals can begin to live and walk in the will of God and gain greater freedom.

[His] word is a lamp for my feet, a light on my path (Psalm 119:105). His word leads us in the way of freedom.

Jesus said we shall know the truth and the truth will set us free (John 8:32). Jesus said of Himself, *'I am the way and the truth and the life'* (John 14:6). I believe it true to say that a person can only be free to the extent that they understand the truth of all Jesus has done and why. The journey of freedom increases as individuals grow in their knowledge and experience of the truth found in Jesus and His word. As truth is accepted by faith, the more it begins to be understood, embraced, and practised, the greater the level of freedom and revelation a person knows, bringing transformation and authority.

I recall giving my life to Jesus, not fully realising all that Jesus had done for me or how that should naturally impact my life. Having been born again I had received power to live differently as well as a new life and identity as a child of

God, yet my lack of understanding and knowledge of this truth meant that I soon found myself back on drugs, and in the grip of its power again. However, sometime later I encountered truth again as Jesus met with me in my room and I once again came face to face with what Jesus had done for me on the cross and why. This encounter led me to a place of understanding more fully what Jesus had done, thus from that moment on I surrendered to Him and made a conscious decision that I would let Jesus take the wheel of my life. I have been on this journey of walking out my freedom for 15 years.

This works best in a loving, supportive community: the church will often focus on freedom ministry in some capacity, with Rehab or specialised recovery groups, which provide support and friendship for others on the same journey. However, a combination of the two will always be the best option. Having others that have walked this path come alongside a recovering addict is also a great source of strength and encouragement. Counselling may be required at stages in the healing process. It is also important to aid individuals in the rebuilding of their lives by helping them to gain and learn new life skills. All of these will serve together to help in the renewal of the mind, restoring dignity, and living substance free.

As those who are called to be His ministers of the gospel (2 Corinthians 3:6) we must remember that we are in a spiritual war and that whilst the spirit is strong the flesh can be weak. This is also where addicts and former addicts can be vulnerable to temptations, defaulting to known coping mechanisms built via trauma or through life, and thus submitting to negative and destructive mindsets that have been formed over time.

As ministers of the gospel, we understand we are also battling with spiritual influences at work in people's lives. That whilst there are natural obstacles and challenges to overcome, continued weaknesses can at times be attributed to spiritual influences operating in people's lives.

With this knowledge we are able to focus not just on the practical help but on spiritual intervention, and not allow the natural difficulties and challenging circumstances to cause us to submit to what we see, rather we take a hold of prayer and apply faith in the name of Jesus. His name that is powerful enough to change lives and break through where we cannot.

- There are also practical things we can aid with:

- Get connected to support groups that deal with the issues

- Get connected to a group in church

- Have a mentor to help set goals, education, work, family, etc.

- Focused discipleship

There will be many battles. The apostle Paul refers to this battle in Romans 12:2. For those caught in addiction this is where one of the greatest battles takes place.

For the weapons of our warfare are not carnal but mighty in God for the pulling down of strongholds, casting down arguments and every high thing that exalts itself against the knowledge of God, bringing every thought into captivity to the obedience of Christ. (2 Corinthians 10:4-5 NKJV)

The object of an individual's addiction has built up strongholds in their mind and reasoning. For example, the need for the fix, to fix their deeper need, or to alleviate their withdrawals. Their dependence upon the substance to function often goes beyond physicality to a powerful belief that restricts their ability to stop. This comes together with other lies about their past and present, ungodly beliefs that keep them bound and imprisoned.

For as [a man] thinks in his heart, so is he. (Proverbs 23:7 NKJV)

The heart and the mind are intrinsically linked: as much as there is a battle for the mind, there is a battle for the heart, for it's a response of the heart that invites Jesus to truly come and transform a person. This is vital, as the degree to which the person surrenders is usually the extent to which you see Christ's influence and subsequent power working in their life.

Whether someone has responded to receive Jesus or not, wounds of the heart and emotional ties to children, partners, and other toxic and non-toxic relationships will be apparent and an obvious distraction. Often the emotions attached to these relationships will be a strong driving force and dictate behaviour and choices. However, they often end up simply feeding the call for drugs in the life of the person caught in addiction.

Sharing the gospel with addicts

Addicts who come into church can often feel stigmatised. It is vital that we seek out the addicts for Jesus, in and outside of the church. Jesus is already at work in their lives and is just waiting for us to partner with what He is doing and wants to do.

When it comes to witnessing, particularly on the streets or to a group, I would recommend that you do not go alone but either as a group or in twos; this way you are able to cover one another in prayer and you will be able to support one another should any situations arise.

Remember you are empowered to be Christ's witness and Christ loves those caught in addiction and wants to reveal Himself.

[Jesus] called unto him the twelve, and began to send them forth by two and two; and gave them power over unclean spirits. (Mark 6:7 KJV, see also Luke 10:1)

I have always found when I pray and expect God to move, He does. He wants us to be available for Him to minister through. He loves to reveal Himself and minister to people.

The Holy Spirit will come upon an individual any time, any place, to reveal God's love and presence.

On one occasion, myself and a friend prayed for a young woman on the street who was in the grip of addiction and chaos. We prayed for her and her situation in the name of Jesus. The Holy Spirit came upon her so powerfully it was all we could do to stop her falling to the ground. When she came to, she was stunned at the experience. In that moment the peace of God and His presence was so strong she could not stop talking about what had just happened. She also recollected many years ago in prison she used to go to chapel and how she often recited Psalm 23. I was able to share with her about Jesus wanting her to trust Him with her whole life. We prayed again and I was able to give her a Bible and encourage her to keep looking to Him.

Again and again, I have witnessed the Holy Spirit break into the most complex situations on the street and heal, fill, and touch. However, we are always looking to connect with the individual and relate to them. From that place we can witness or offer prayer, and it is often then that they encounter the presence of Jesus.

When engaging and sharing the gospel keep alert: one ear to what's going on with the person and one ear to the Spirit. Paying attention enables you to gain insight and wisdom to where someone may be in their journey and how to approach and engage with them and co-operate with the Spirit's leading.

Prayer is key to hearing and seeing what the Lord is doing and to seeing people encounter the power and presence of Jesus. When in twos it also enables one person to be quietly praying whilst the other is talking.

- Lean on the Holy Spirit to guide you

- Don't complicate things

- Don't use religious language

- Don't argue

- Share the gospel and how Christ died to bring freedom

- If they are not ready to receive Jesus, pray your best prayer of blessing over them

Important tips when ministering

Giving:

How and what you give is important and can be a grey area. Do not give cash and do not allow yourself to be used to help maintain a lifestyle, although occasionally it is good to help in a situation where you believe the Lord is leading you to, and where you discern it is ok to do so.

It is important that you apply wisdom and understand that it is not wise to make yourself vulnerable in these situations as these environments can at times be chaotic and unpredictable. Make sure that you are not alone.

Boundaries:

Boundaries and consistency in maintaining them are important. The addict's tendency is to want to manipulate, push, and extend those boundaries in all areas. It is necessary that you set your boundaries in truth and love and that you remain steadfast in maintaining them. In most instances the addict is driven by their need, and their primary goal is to get a fix. However, maintaining boundaries will eventually produce respect alongside a sense of stability and security, even if you experience a kick-back at first. Many will lack the knowledge of good and healthy boundaries so explaining what your boundaries are and why they are there is helpful. Self-awareness is also important to help you develop and maintain good boundaries. Awareness regarding your own character, including strengths and weaknesses and any past trauma, will to help you to focus on your own boundaries. For example, if you find it difficult to say no, or perhaps by nature you are a rescuer, you may have to be mindful of your expectations and of making promises to others that may become unmanageable.

Sharing the Gospel:

Don't be a hero, and don't push when someone is resisting or does not want to know or engage with what you're inviting them into. They may be carrying baggage, hurt, and frustrations which at times may be a block. Wait for another appointed time. Love them and be gracious, be considerate about where they are in their journey.

It is important to maintain love, faith, hope, and confidence in the gospel. Don't allow any negative reactions, rejection, or what seems like no progress to cloud the truth of the gospel and God's word and cause you to doubt, lose heart, or shrink back from faith in Jesus and His gospel.

Sharing the gospel in both deed and word is powerful. Some will be ready and open to receive Jesus into their life immediately, yet for others it may take many years before they get a breakthrough. Either way, we are those called to love and bring this message of faith, hope, and love into people's lives and lift them up.

Love never gives up. Love never fails, bears all things, hopes all things, endures all things. (See 1 Corinthians 13)

Even in the face of what seems impossible, *with God all things are possible.*

Deliverance and spirits of addiction

With the increase and rise of mental health issues and the obvious need for deliverance in people's lives, we need the gift of discernment to distinguish where deliverance, healing, or help for a mental health condition is required. However, in most instances an addict is likely to have been affected in all these areas. Depression, anxiety, fear, and PTSD are often found in an addict but are different to a diagnosis of a specific mental health condition, such as bipolar disorder, for example.

This is an incredibly complex area, one in which we should walk carefully and with the Holy Spirit, seeking discernment to ensure that we do not go ahead on our own and create additional problems. When someone is fragile of mind and you are still not sure whilst seeking the Lord, it is perhaps best to quietly pray and ask for God's peace over them.

Spirits of addiction:

These spirits often promise a world of escapism from reality for the person who is trying to cope with life. When a person turns to escapism, it can open them up to addiction which grows into a bondage where spirits of addiction are involved, and it seems nearly impossible to break free (without deliverance, that is).

It is important to note that with any addict there are likely to be various spiritual influences at work in their life.

Do not attempt deliverance with someone that is an addict who has not received salvation.

If they have just been saved do not attempt specific deliverance unless the Holy Spirit tells you and you are living a clean life. Do not do it alone. Make sure that you are accountable and that you have mature Christians to pray with you during and afterwards.

When an unclean spirit goes out of a man, he goes through dry places, seeking rest, and finds none. Then he says, 'I will return to my house from which I came.' And when he comes, he finds it empty, swept, and put in order. Then he goes and takes with him seven other spirits more wicked than himself, and they enter and dwell there; and the last state of that man is worse than the first. So shall it also be with this wicked generation. (Matthew 12:43-45 NKJV)

There may be occasions whereby someone wants to be free, but they are not willing or ready to give up certain things that have given spirits legal ground in their lives. In such instances spirits may be more stubborn to leave, and if they are cast out, will come back with a vengeance because they have permission to be there.

Important questions to ask before addressing any demonic influences:

- Are they saved? Have they been born again and committed their life to Jesus?
- Are they willing to give up anything necessary to maintain their freedom?
- Are they willing to seek, follow, and stay close to Jesus?
- Are they ready to engage with the word of God and an ongoing relationship with Jesus to maintain their freedom?

It is important that the individual has reached a place where they recognise their need for Jesus and all that He has done on the cross to reconcile them to the Father and His purposes for them.

Once you have led them to the Lord Jesus and you are confident that they want to be free, you can pray for freedom. Below is a simple way I might pray to address spirits of addiction if I discerned this was the right thing to do. In my own journey, the first time I prayed to receive Christ I went back to using. The second time I more fully understood what Jesus had done for me and, after repenting and praying again, I was completely set free from the spirit of drug addiction.

How to pray:

Once the individual has received Jesus as their Lord and understand what they have prayed, if I trust this is sincere I will gently ask them to look at me and ask them if they really want to be free. If they say yes, I will address the spirit of addiction and command it to leave. Looking them in the eye and asking them to look at me, I simply take authority and say, *'Spirit of addiction, I command you to leave right now in the name of Jesus.'*

I do this gently. There is no need to raise you voice, your authority comes from your relationship and union with Jesus; this is the foundational truth that authority flows from. It is your confidence in Jesus and His ability to deliver.

I then pray that the person be filled with the Holy Spirit and speak God's peace over them.

Following the prayer, I would ask them how they feel. Did they sense anything? I would then reassure them that Jesus has set them free. I would share a scripture that I felt was apt for them as an encouragement in their new-found freedom. I would also seek to follow them up or connect them with a Christian, church, or another Christian group to help them continue in their journey.

Finding freedom is a process and there are several keys to aid this process: repentance, forgiveness, truth, and sometimes praying over generation sins if there has been an obvious display in their family history, which has proved a weakness down the family line.

Remember:

- No one chooses to become an addict.
- Poor lifestyle choices born out of brokenness and sin lead to addiction.
- For many addicts, drugs and alcohol provide a means of escape and thus they self-medicate using drugs and alcohol, possibly to deal with pain, trauma, and responsibilities that they don't know how to handle. Often there are multiple reasons and influences at work prior to addiction.
- Spiritual help is a necessary part of the course to healing.

However, despite all that, we must not forget that Jesus delivered the demoniac man in an instance with a simple command; it was a power encounter. When someone has a true experience of Jesus in this way in their lives, it is powerful and life changing.

Likewise, deliverance can come in stages as someone receives Christ then begins to surrender to Him and His word.

Jesus said to the people who believed in him, 'You are truly my disciples if you remain faithful to my teachings. And you will know the truth, and the truth will set you free.' (John 8:31-32 NLT)

So, it is important that you adhere to the voice of God lest you try to be the one to save and rescue, perhaps doing more harm than good.

Whilst the spirit comes alive to God at salvation, sanctification (aligning with God's word) is an ongoing process, and godliness and healing are lifelong journeys. It is important to be aware that beyond any physical improvement and obvious giftings, that the healing of those who have experienced years of addiction and trauma can be a complex and lengthy process when it comes to walking in full freedom.

When an addict makes a choice to invite Jesus into their life

Their spirit comes alive unto God.

And if Christ is in you, the body is dead because of sin, but the Spirit is life because of righteousness. (Romans 8:10 NKJV; see also Ephesians 2)

The apostle Paul's instruction in Romans is to *not let sin control the way you live; do not give in to sinful desires. Do not let any part of your body become an instrument of evil to serve sin. Instead, give yourselves completely to God, for you were dead, but now you have new life. So use your whole body as an instrument to do what is right for the glory of God* (Romans 6:12-13 NLT).

For most that come to faith in Christ the spirit is willing but the flesh can be weak, particularly when an addict remains in the same challenging situation and circumstances. Therefore, it is important to understand that patience and grace is required while allowing the Holy Spirit to change a person.

Alongside this, be aware of challenges that seem obstructive and their need for other sources of help, or for support more able to meet their specific needs. It is important that you or another party walks alongside them, teaching them to live in an ongoing relationship with God and that, despite the challenges of life, they can still know Him.

Quite often a change of environment will enable the individual time to engage with what God is doing away from the enormous temptation that they will face if they continue in the same situation, surrounded by the same people. However, for many they will still have to wrestle with temptations if they move, and this will differ from person to person.

Applying the word of God and understanding what is happening will help and empower the individual to make the right choices.

The temptations in your life are no different from what others experience. And God is faithful. He will not allow the temptation to be more than you can stand. When you are tempted, he will show you a way out so that you can endure. (1 Corinthians 10:13 NLT)

Alongside this, use other distractions and tools to help the individual's mind engage with activities and goals. This is an important benefit of love and community to help strengthen, hold accountable, and encourage.

Breaking habits

A habit is born out of repetition of a routine or behaviour, then it can become almost involuntary by nature; it can be a lifestyle, response, thought pattern.

Popular opinion is that it takes 21 days to form a habit, so it requires a conscious realisation and new practice to change this.

Dr Caroline Leaf is a cognitive neuroscientist with a PhD in Communication Pathology, specialising in metacognitive and cognitive neuropsychology. She writes that the same principle can be applied to undo a habit or change the wrong way of thinking, which she refers to as toxic thoughts. However, as she rightly notes, this replacement of thought with the word of God regarding the behaviour will need ongoing nurturing for it will take 63 days to be actualised.[2] Thus, even when God brings a revelation of truth, there needs to be a coming into agreement in that area of the mind for it to become embedded in the heart and for the truth to bear fruit and be effective in the life of the individual.

Those who are addicted, or have been when they receive Christ, may either be delivered instantly or over time. Yet all will need to change habits, break free from unhealthy ties and associations (toxic, abusive, manipulative, and co-dependent relationships) if they are going to stand a chance of sustaining their new-found freedom and walk out their new life in Christ.

2. Dr Caroline Leaf, *Switch on Your Brain* (Grand Rapids, MI: Baker Books, 2013), p152.

Soul realm

It is important to note that when they receive Christ, the individual's spirit comes alive to God (Ephesians 2:5), yet their soul takes time to heal and will find the most conflict. The soul comprises of the heart, the mind, and the will.

This is where the renewal of the mind, the healing of a wounded soul, and submission to Jesus is all being worked out. The sanctification process takes time (1 Thessalonians 4:3).

Often wounds have been an opening for demonic influence to gain access to trouble, oppress, and sow lies. Jesus is the wonderful counsellor who has given us the Holy Spirit who searches out all things and takes us on that journey of sanctification, repentance, cleansing, and submission to God. This takes time and can happen as the individual engages with the Lord and partners with the Holy Spirit. This will require patience and understanding as this part of a person has been shaped their whole lives by brokenness, alternate world views, and self-seeking and rebellious behaviours. Therefore, we will often see an individual soar spiritually when they are born again, yet possibly continue to operate in rebellion, anger, and be overwhelmed by fear and negative emotions and thoughts. There will be a root that needs to be dealt with through repentance, forgiveness, breaking of curses (words and generational), thus enabling these areas where there have been destructive and negative influences at work to be removed, at which point we can close the door and choose to submit to God.

Mind

It is here in the mind where ungodly beliefs and strongholds are formed.

For me personally, I had grown up believing that something was wrong with me and that I was the problem, so I always carried the belief that I was damaged goods.

Where your mind goes, your heart follows; one affects the other (Proverbs 24:7).

This affected many of the poor choices I made in relation to what I would permit into my life and the decision I made to go into sex work to fund my addiction.

When I became born again, I knew Jesus valued me but I have had to continually renew my mind and press past negative emotions attached to that when it comes to how others see me.

Again, this is one of the reasons why the apostle Paul says that our minds need to be transformed, renewed into a new way of thinking (come into alignment with the truth), that we may prove God and His perfect and acceptable will for and in our lives (Romans 12:2).

There is a battle for the mind that goes on not just for the addict but for all believers. We need to teach people the truth and how to obey and walk in that truth in taking every thought captive to the obedience of Christ.

We destroy every proud obstacle that keeps people from knowing God. We capture their rebellious thoughts and teach them to obey Christ. (2 Corinthians 10:5 NLT)

Teaching, walking and submitting to the truth will ultimately see the addict receive healing, freedom, and overcome the battle that takes place in the mind. However, it is important to note, somethings come quickly through revelation of the Spirit, yet some strongholds need to be broken down and that can take time.

In her book *Switch on Your Brain*, Dr Caroline Leaf talks about the power of the brain and its capacity to rewire itself. She makes these points:

As we think, we change the physical nature of our brain. As we consciously direct our thinking, so we can wire out toxic thoughts. *'It is with our phenomenal minds we choose to develop the spiritual part of who we are.'*[3]

Good thoughts = Good choices = Healthy thoughts

Toxic thinking = Toxic choices = Toxic thinking

---

3. Leaf, *Switch on Your Brain*, p21.

You are not a victim of your biology, you can change.

Your thoughts become physical substances in your brain – your thoughts change the matter of your brain.[4]

You are designed to recognise and choose the right things to think about.

Each morning when a person wakes up they have new, baby nerve cells born inside their brain. The process of removing bad thoughts and rewiring new ones is called neurogenesis.[5]

Great is his faithfulness; his mercies begin afresh each morning. (Lamentations 3:23)

Every day we get to choose life!

Will

This is where the individual relinquishes the driving seat of their lives and learns to trust and surrender to Jesus and His will and word. This happens progressively and to varying degrees along the way for each individual. Resistance in an area of their life limits all that God wants to do. Some resistance may be through rebellion but other times it will be due to fears, mistrust, and old mindsets or self-

---

4. Leaf, *Switch on Your Brain*, p21.
5. Leaf, *Switch on Your Brain*, p24.

preservation. All individuals will struggle in different areas when it comes to their will.

It is with the will the individual chooses to partner with the Holy Spirit and agree with God's word, even when it seems contrary to how they feel. This can take time. Gradually they learn to walk by faith and trust in the Lord's goodness, unfailing love, and character as He shows Himself faithful.

The will involves submission to God. The extent to which people are able to trust may also affect their ability to trust God. However, as they see God's faithfulness, that trust will increase. For many people they will have a catalogue of responses that are embedded in them to respond to the world around them, to cope and protect themselves.

If they are willing to partner with God and the work of the Holy Spirit in them, God will be able to accomplish much more in a shorter space of time.

It will begin one step at a time; conscious steps and choices despite challenges and feelings to the contrary.

Change can only come when the individual is willing; trying to force someone will never bear lasting fruit and change.

Fear is also not a good motivator. Whilst presenting truth in love can be about a godly fear, manmade fear will only become a snare producing legalism and not a living, dynamic relationship with Jesus Christ.

Heart

The heart is the home of our emotions.

Jesus came to heal the broken in heart and bind up their wounds. You will often find that an undealt with wound is at the root of the choice to use. Then as a result of the choices the addict makes, comes more heartache.

Often emotions have been damaged, or negative emotions and associations have been buried deep within a person. These emotions will have been a driving force in their life and in the choices that they have made.

In my former life, my emotions ruled me. I was like a roller coaster, and they dictated what I thought and believed about myself. They were my compass for life, decisions, and beliefs. One day, as I was reading the Bible, I realised my emotions did not have to dictate my life but I could choose what to think about. This was a huge revelation and gave me back some control in a godly way over my life; it transformed my life from there on. I did not need to submit to the emotions but could choose differently, regardless of how I felt.

Those undealt with old or new wounds and interpretations will affect the way an individual perceives themselves, others, and the world around them. This is where the enemy gains ground through unforgiveness and resentment and can plant lies.

The thief comes only to steal and kill and destroy; I have come that they may have life, and have it to the full. (John 10:10)

It is always good when ministering to the emotions and those areas that seem to provoke an emotional response to get to the root of the issue. Then, if that person is ready, they can receive healing from the Lord Jesus.

Wounds will manifest in many ways, so getting to the root will help in dealing with any other behaviours that are showing themselves. For example, if someone has undergone a trauma, they may overcompensate in areas, or became aggressive, defensive, unable to communicate, seek attention, and so on.

It is also important to guide the individual when they are ready to seek healing to get to that root.

Always ask the Holy Spirit to guide in these instances, for Jesus alone is the wonderful counsellor and is able to bind up the wounds of the broken.

An open door is a place where someone's life has been opened to the enemy's influence: inherited curses; fear; generational sins including sins of the flesh (repeated sins, such as anger, jealousy, pride, rebellion, sexual, etc.); illness and accidents (physical trauma and weakening due to illness, prescribed medications); emotional trauma; trances; occult involvement.

The keys for leading the person into healing are: repenting, forgiving, and taking back any legal right the enemy has gained in their life through walking in sin and/or coming into agreement with his lies. Repenting and rejecting these and submitting to God enables us to close the doors opened to the enemy's influence. This means removing the legal right of the enemy to torment or to hold them captive, and praying for the individual to be filled with the Holy Spirit. This will release them from any demonic influence. It must be said again, though, that a healing of the emotions and renewal of the mind is an ongoing process for walking out complete freedom. In some instances it may happen immediately but usually it will take some time.

Sent ones

Jesus ministers to the afflicted and the outcasts. He seeks them out and He never turns anyone away when they come to Him. He ministers in grace, truth, and love in such a way that it demands a response.

As His sons and daughters our mandate is that of Christ: we are anointed to do the works of Jesus. Let us remain bold, steadfast, and not grow weary in reaching and ministering to the addicts as, in due time, we will reap a harvest. Take heart, it is Christ in you that does the work as we partner with His Holy Spirit in us.

Declaration

The spirit of the Lord is on me, because he has anointed me to proclaim good news to the poor. He has sent me to proclaim freedom for the prisoners and recovery of sight for the blind, to set the oppressed free, to proclaim the year of the Lord's favour. (Luke 4:18-19)

Places to contact for help

Organisations and Charities

Mind (Mental health, addiction, suicide, self-harm, eating disorders)

Call: 0300 123 3393

Web: www.mind.org.uk/information-support/helplines

Email: info@mind.org.uk

Text: SHOUT to 85258

Teen Challenge UK (Rehab)

Call: 01664 822 221 (Willoughby House); 01269 844 114 (Hope House)

Web: www.teenchallenge.org.uk/about

Email: admissions@teenchallenge.org.uk

Ellel Ministries UK and Ireland

Call: +44 (0)1524 751651)

Web: www.ellel.org/uk/

Email: info@ellelministries.org Hello@Ellel.org

Hope Centre Cwmbran (Rehab)

Call: 0300 1024579

Web: www.hopecm.co.uk

Victory Outreach Manchester (Rehab)

Call: 0161 737 6624

Web: www.vomanchester.org.uk

Email: info@vomanchester.org.uk

Refuge (Domestic violence)

Call: 0808 2000 247

Web: www.nationaldahelpline.org.uk

Rape Crisis (Rape)

Call: 0808 802 9999

Web: www.rapecrisis.org.uk

Support Line (Rape, suicide, self-harm)

Call: 01708 765 200

Web: www.supportline.org.uk/contact-us

Email: info@supportline.org.uk

Rethink (Suicide, self-harm)

Call: 0808 801 0525

Web: www.rethink.org

Unseen (Modern slavery)

Call: 08000 121 700

Web: www.unseenuk.org

Beloved (Sex industry)

Call: 07541 366 577

Web: www.beloved.org.uk

Email: hello@beloved.org.uk

Beyond The Streets (Sex industry)

Call: 0800 133 7870

Web: www.beyondthestreets.org.uk

Email: support@beyondthestreets.org.uk

Samaritans

Call: 116 123

Web: www.samaritans.org

Email: jo@samaritans.org

Shalom Recovery Training:

Do you want to support people to recover from addiction and mental ill-health so they can live a life of wellness and wholeness? Whether you're already doing this or just starting out, Shalom Recovery Training offer their experience to help support you to become a recovery-equipped community.

Web: https://shalomrecoverytraining.carrd.co

Email: shalomrecoverytraining@gmail.com

Abused • Addicted • Free

The inspiring true story of Trudy Makepeace

He grabbed my throat with one hand and pushed the edge of a blade to my neck with the other. "One wrong move and I'll cut your throat!" I felt the cold edge of the knife against my flesh. I shivered as he pushed the tip deeper into my skin. "Who do you think you are?" he shouted. Fear gripped my heart as he traced the blade across my throat; it could all be over in seconds.

Months later when Trudy Makepeace arrived at the girl's home in Tredegar, a staff member on duty at the time wondered how she was still alive. "Trudy was skin and bone, with fear in her eyes I have never seen someone so destroyed by drugs."

'Addicted Abused Free, conveys Trudy's personal story and I truly commend her for her courage and desire to share it. Yet, it is not just her story that is remarkable, but also God's story; a story that clearly expresses His heart.'

Fiona Fallon, National Programme Director, Teen Challenge UK

'Few autobiographies I have read have been written with such transparent honesty as this powerful book from Trudy Makepeace. I fully recommend this book.'

John Glass, Elim General Superintendent 2000-2016 and Chair of Council, Evangelical Alliance 2014-2018

'Trudy's story is a story many can identify with, but it's so much more. This book will change many lives because it exposes a profound truth in every heart: that we are all looking for the right thing but in all the wrong places.'

Rev Simon Foster, Elim Minister, Elim National Leadership Team 2008-2018

'What a story! Trudy's journey shows that there is always hope, even when the odds are against you from the off. I totally endorse this book. Buy it, then fasten your seat belt!'

Barry Woodward, Author of Once an Addict & Director of Proclaim Trust

For more information go to:

https://www.malcolmdown.co.uk/abused-addicted-free

https://www.trudymakepeace.com

https://www.instagram.com/trudy.makepeace

https://www.facebook.com/trudy.makepeace